TIGER

Tiger

Cliff Forshaw

Happen*Stance*

Poems © Cliff Forshaw, 2011
Cover image © Gillian Beaton, 2011
ISBN 978-1-905939-62-6
All rights reserved.

Sequence series, 5.

Acknowledgements:
Thanks are due to editors of the following publications, in which earlier versions of parts of this sequence first appeared: *Light on Don Bank: Fifteen Years of Live Poets*, eds Danny Gardner & Sue Hicks (Live Poets' Press, Sydney, 2006); *Poetry Wales*.

Also by Cliff Forshaw:
- *Wake* (Flarestack Poets, 2009, joint-winner of the 2009 Flarestack Pamphlet Prize)
- *A Ned Kelly Hymnal* (A Paper Special Edition, Cherry on the Top Press, Sheffield, 2008)
- *Trans* (The Collective Press, Wales, 2005)
- *The Dade County Book of the Dead* (National Poetry Foundation, 1995)
- *Strange Tongues* (Weasel, 1994)
- *Esau's Children* (National Poetry Foundation, 1991)
- *Himalayan Fish* (Peacock Books, Orissa, India, 1991)

Printed by The Dolphin Press
www.dolphinpress.co.uk
Published in 2010 by Happen*Stance*
21 Hatton Green, Glenrothes, Fife KY7 4SD
nell@happenstancepress.com
www.happenstancepress.com

Orders:
Individual pamphlets £4.00 (includes UK P&P).
Please make cheques payable to Happen*Stance* or order through PayPal in the website shop.

Many thanks to Joe Bugden and The Tasmanian Writers' Centre, Hobart for their hospitality during a fruitful period as International Writer-in-Residence, 2004. Thanks also to Hawthornden Castle International Retreat for Writers, Lasswade, Scotland, for its hospitality and for allowing me to return for a second productive fellowship in 2009.

Tiger

The thylacine, or 'Tasmanian Tiger', the world's largest marsupial carnivore, originally native to continental Australia, Tasmania and New Guinea, was declared extinct in 1986. Though deliberately hunted to the brink of extinction throughout the nineteenth and early twentieth century, it was given the status of protected species two months before the last documented Tiger died in 1936 in a Hobart zoo.

Attempts to clone the thylacine, using DNA from preserved specimens, have so far proved unsuccessful. The Tiger has assumed a popular mythic status in Tasmania, with unconfirmed sightings continuing to this day.

*For Les Wicks,
Oz poet and good mate,
who first suggested Tasmania.*

Loop

62 seconds of the extinct Thylacine or Tasmanian Tiger on film.

Within the box, it growls, it twists,
scowls through its repertoire of tricks,
ignores the camera—or gurns up close, turns
again, to flop, to gnaw that paw-trapped bone.

It paces out its trap of light; one hundred reps,
while hindquarters zither bars of sun.
You saw. You see. What claws cage's mesh, hangs stretched
as if to take the measure of itself.

And what we've got is what was shot:
short clips, fragments caught and stitched
together in a loop of black and white.

Nine lives? Not quite. It's down. It's out.
It's on its feet and born again. Like a repetition
compulsion, like . . . like reincarnated light.

Tarraleah . . . Wayatinah . . .

Barcode

Extinct, this creature's everywhere
from CD sleeves to bottled beer.
With trademarked stripes, it zebras out
between the gums' abstracted light.
They've even tigered my hired Mazda's plate.
Everything's branded. *Tasmania—your natural state.*

Now you see them. Now they're gone.
Did this Tiger's go-faster stripes
aid recognition in the loping pack?

Eucalypts, eucalypts—at speed,
late sun flickers through those trees:
at the tarmac edge, off-cuts of fur, strange weeds.

Billboards, stores along the newly-metalled road:
ironic ads, that hide's barcode.

. . . Catagunya, Lake Repulse . . .

Old Hairy

And here he is, 'Old Hairy',
red and skinny, tough as boots,
four thousand years old if he's a day;
forever flat out and in pursuit

of . . . whatever. The chase goes on and on.
That endless prey's his last: the one
that's slipped its skeleton through a crack in stone,
a white shadow in the rock that's worn him down
to skin and bone. That's skin? That's bone?

(To the south, earth shifts, Tassie breaks free:
distant cousins in cold high woods, cut off by sea.)

Dry as parchment, brittle as sticks:
Mummified mainland thylacine,
found base of shaft, Nullarbor Plain, '66.

． . . *Zeehan, Strahan, Teepookana* . . .

Quirk

Next to extinct stripes, the stuttered screen:
one skull, one larger skeleton, a box
of assorted bones and one small stuffed thylacine.

Crouched here, what looks foetal, but's been marked
in ink: *Pouch young—before 1910,*
almost hairless, pickled in a jar.
You think of what this means, then look again.

Closer, where that curiously upturned snout
sniffs at its bung of dead trapped air,
a few surprisingly wiry bristles sprout,
magnified by the glass's curve.

Above the brownish bevel, the century's dripped white.
Eyes closed, it noses out the hang of things. Just what
has pierced that lid with long thin fangs? Stalactites.

                              . . . Marakoopa, Crotty Dam . . .

Star

Pouch young. But that familiar foetal curve
keeps on deceiving right down to this tail's curl.
No stripes. It's just a flourish underlining
the space that's signally left unsigned. No god
has scratched his mark. Here's work-in-progress still.

Marsupium meaning 'pouch', much like the Greek
thylakos, ditto one in leather. What light gets in
stains it brown as old veneer;
what you've got's gone Dutch with death. Still-life.
I'm thinking *nature morte*: a flitch of bacon,
hung pheasant, hare, a jug of flattening beer

when I see, quicksilvered against what's aborted, jarred,
my reflection caught upon that quirk,
light from that screen turning us all to silent stars.

... *Lileah, Nabageena* ...

Road kill

What *is* this stuff with tails? This slump of fur
that mimes the body's weight, intimates
the slow tug of earth that gets us all. You swerve
to miss these weird speed bumps, glimpse
a forested ridge in the marginalia of the road,
a premonition of mountains in that hump.

Each is a map to what still lies, lies still
—yet moves—now like a wave, now flat-out:
roadstone's quake, asphalt fever, that tremor
shivering towards you through the heat-haze,
visions of angels skating on the shimmer.

Blind bend. Horn. The dopplered blare
through ears and car and ribs. Road train.
Chained logs, knee-trembled, hovering on compressed air.

. . . Savage River, Blackguard's Hill . . .

In inverted commas

Others are Disney-flat, out-run cartoons
who've failed to burrow into tarmac,
who've found it far too hard, too black.
At this one's mouth, a speech-balloon
where asphalt's slick and almost pink,
as if someone's scrubbed long and hard at red
daubed words, the rumour's near indelible ink.

Haunches, muddied pelts, dithered paws,
little fangs gnawing on the camber;
snouts punctuated by inverted commas of claws:
irony or speech marks, a question mark of tail,
rising like the intonation you get round here.

So 'politely' put. But a question nonetheless.
It demands sometime, sometime quite soon, you answer *Yes*.

. . . Cradle Mountain, Pieman River . . .

Possum

Now something's listening out for the *ute*'s hissed tread.
Forests. The further in, the more you get.
Possums, not playing at it, they're really dead.
Now that the Tassie Tiger's gone, the devils
are in league with us. Plastinated Penguin
(pub. lib. & overdue) says: *Thylacine males,
like Tas. Devils (their closest extant relatives),
had pseudo-pouches to protect their testicles.*

The rumour's going round (you heard it here
from those that heard it first) that once you've done
your stretch you're out of here. *They lie in wait.*
Inside time, we also serve who only . . .
The truth's out there. It's on the outside where
you'll need all the balls you think that you, your family, got.

                              . . . Misery Plateau, Gates of Hell . . .

The bottom line

Tarraleah, Wayatinah, Catagunya, Lake Repulse,
Zeehan, Strahan, Teepookana, Marakoopa, Crotty Dam,
Lileah, Nabageena, Savage River, Blackguard's Hill.
Out of Queenstown, down the Franklin,
at Cradle Mountain, the Walls of Jerusalem;
one on the banks of Pieman River,
past the place they named Corinna;
unconfirmed sightings at Misery Plateau, Gates of Hell.

On the road to Wayatinah,
hard to tell in scratchy rain
if what stripes the dusk's a mangy
dog, its ribs all chiaroscuro hunger,
or weather rubbing landscape out.

Or the passing place, where headlights catch
what crosses track—that flash glimpsed in the paddock,
head down low, salaamed to dirt,
bowing or praying. What you see at first
is resolved, from something grumbling an argument
with the earth itself, to some long-snouted thing
with life between its teeth, its dragged-back iffy twitch.

For days, that nervous stuff all looks like prey:
a lope that's dopplered through the boles of trees,
is *there . . . there . . . there,* is disappeared.
And all around, the bottom line goes:
Tarraleah, Wayatinah, Catagunya . . .

Past the place they named Corinna,
what you hear is ghosts, ghosts, ghosts. . . .

Thylacinus Cynocephalus

"Caught kangaroo and killed one hyaena on the sandy beach. The hyaena is called mannalargenna (east coast), cabbarone-nenner, by the Cape Grimm, lowenin, by Jenny (north coast) clinner, by the Cape Portland warternooner, by the Brune cannenner, and by the Oyster Bay lartner..."
George Augustus Robinson, diary entry, 30 August, 1833.

Zebra Opossum. Zebra Wolf.
Tasmanian Zebra. Marsupial Wolf.
Striped Wolf. Tiger Wolf. Tasmanian Wolf.
Lagunta, corinna, laoonana, ka-nunnah

Van Diemen's Land Tiger. Tasmanian Tiger.
Bulldog Tiger. Greyhound Tiger.
Hyaena. Native Hyaena. Opossum Hyaena.
Lagunta, corinna, laoonana, ka-nunnah

Dingo. Tasmanian Dingo. Panther.
Dog-Headed Pouched-Dog.
Pouched-Dog with Wolf Head.
Lagunta, corinna, laoonana, ka-nunnah

Didelphis cynocephala (1806),
Thylacinus cynocephalus (1824).
Excursion into sub-order Dasyuromorphia:
Dasyurus cynocephalus (1810),
from *dasyrus* meaning 'shaggy tail'.
Lagunta, corinna, laoonana, ka-nunnah

I've got you on the tip of my tongue.
You've got me under your skin.
Dog-Faced Dasyrus. Dog-Faced Opossum.
Lagunta, corinna, laoonana, ka-nunnah

Corinna could mean Brave, Corinna could be Fearless.
Wurrawanna Corinna, Great Ghost Tiger.
Lagunta, corinna, laoonana, ka-nunnah,
lowenin, cabbarrone-nenner, mannalargenna,
clinner, warternooner, lartner, cannenner

Shot

Just off the Hobart wharves,
  saw him sizing up his prey:
a head stuck up upon a wall
shot in silvered monochrome
  in an internet café.

That pair of burning eyes,
  that famous wolfish grin:
another extinct Tasmanian,
  that damned smooth Errol Flynn.

Just up the road, the Museum loops
  through enigmatic clips,
while this charismatic *loup garou*
  smacks predatory lips.

Errol left smooth talkies,
  but our star of silver screen
was more laconic Valentino:
  that damned elusive Thylacine!

Errol's dad was biologist
  Professor T. T. Flynn,
who dreamed of a Tiger sanctuary
  (though he also flogged their skins).

Now a pair of ghostly Tigers
  guard Tassie's coat-of-arms,
as if heraldic thylacines
  could bark the next alarm.

Not rampant, couchant or dormant,
    nor mordant—for the dead don't bite—
those state-employed marsupials
    have long given up the fight.

And if, at night, the forest gurns
    with unearthly shrieks and growls,
that's just our municipal cleaning devils.
    There's hygiene in them howls.

The last Tiger in captivity
    died back in '36
though in the wild a few lived on
    with sightings in the sticks.

And half a century later,
    though officially extinct,
the odd backwoodsman sees one,
    after a few stiff drinks.

I heard that scientists in Sydney
    got up to their old tricks:
took a foetus kept in alcohol
    since 1866.

The DNA's high-quality,
    geneticists had said.
If replication works, we'll raise
    the Tiger from the dead.

But until some Frankenstein turns on
    the lights in Jurassic Park,
we're doomed to burn the fossils up
    for fuel in the dark.

Heard tell that when he took
    that famous Tiger footage
The cameraman David Fleay
    took a nasty bite on the buttocks.

Just off the Hobart wharves,
    saw him sizing up his prey:
a head stuck up upon a wall
shot in silvered monochrome
    in an internet café.

That pair of burning eyes,
    that famous wolfish grin:
another extinct Tasmanian,
    that damned smooth Errol Flynn.

Notes:

A link to the short film which inspired 'Loop' (page 9) can be found on Cliff Forshaw's website (www.cliff-forshaw.co.uk).

Thylacinus Cynocephalus:
In *The Last Tasmanian Tiger,* 2002, Robert Paddle points out that the common but incorrect translation as "the dog-headed pouched-dog" is both inelegant and "borders upon the stupid and crass."